G

Klara du Plessis

Khashayar "Kess" Mohammadi

Palimpsest Press
1171 Eastlawn Ave.
Windsor, Ontario. N8S 3J1
www.palimpsestpress.ca

Printed and bound in Canada
Cover design and book typography by Ellie Hastings
Edited by Jim Johnstone

Palimpsest Press would like to thank the Canada Council for the Arts and
the Ontario Arts Council for their support of our publishing program.
We also acknowledge the assistance of the Government of Ontario
through the Ontario Book Publishing Tax Credit.

A **Anstruther Books**

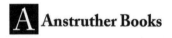

Canada

LIBRARY AND ARCHIVES CANADA CATALOGUING IN PUBLICATION

TITLE: G = Kh / Klara du Plessis, Khashayar "Kess" Mohammadi
OTHER TITLES: Kh
NAMES: Du Plessis, Klara, 1988- author.
        Mohammadi, Khashayar, 1994- author.
DESCRIPTION: 880-01 "Kh" in title statement is transliterated from the
Persian. | Poems in English; include some text in Afrikaans and Persian.
IDENTIFIERS: Canadiana (print) 2023048418
            Canadiana (ebook) 20230484565

ISBN 9781990293542 (SOFTCOVER)
ISBN 9781990293559 (EPUB)
CLASSIFICATION: LCC PS8607.U17 G22 2023 | DDC C811/.6—DC23

Contents

زبان

پروتز

Even in cursive there are gaps in the script,
tiny gateways for the body to take off and leave.
Total entity of the human anatomy,
the illusion of the gatekeeper's arm,
the gatekeeper's leg, the torso sentinel
pretending there's no single pore
that opens its microscopic mouth
through the skin in an unseeable slit of light,
through organs and out back.
Print writing is less dishonest.
The hand lifts between letters.
Dots and lines hover and intersect,
but retain occasional autonomy.
Flickers of text, dust, and ink, composite in unity,
relax into the hospitality of meaning.

---

protese پروتز *(Persian) prosthesis*

Prostese

Prosthesis includes the argumentative stature
of thesis / *tesis* / thesis
being the unstressed syllable of a metrical foot,
putting its foot down and lifting its foot up
in sewing's soft gesture.
The whole body pedals as if life
depends on riding away from itself,
ridding itself of itself.
Dots hover in proximity / incompletion   پروتز
prosthesis /
all these sonic lookalikes, sounded out as *protese* / *prostese* / *prostesis*
protest in their italics, in the name of independence,
of a poetess picking up her feminized identity
and throwing it over her shoulders
like a light that casts shadow for her shoes to cool in.

---

tesis (Afrikaans) thesis
protese پروتز (Persian) prosthesis
protese (Afrikaans) prosthesis
prostese (Afrikaans) prosthesis
prostesis (Afrikaans) prosthesis

Kuns-

Art is the first limb of artificial.
Prosthetic rosetta
pinned under the chin of every bilingual dictionary.
Affect situates itself in the arena of interstice
and ossifies, wringing out bones, skeletal
knowledge of equivalence.

Kuns is art.
Kuns- is artificial.
In a language that writes a composite script
for loss (*kunsbeen, kunsarm*)
grief loosens into attachment, the opening, the nothing,
the –ing.

If the prefix is all that is left
and the clip-on body buffs itself up
into a credible suffix,
the middle radiates a quiet space,
meditates on the craft of every fingertip
that taps out text with the force of eternal resonance
and the haptic paradox of proximity.

---

kuns (Afrikaans) art
kuns- (Afrikaans) artificial
kunsbeen (Afrikaans) prosthetic leg
kunsarm (Afrikaans) prosthetic arm

Tongs

In the phantom margins of this book,
زبان tongue, visually extending language
with two movable arms joined at the head,
waving their sleeves haplessly
in the direction of meaning.
What is the word for *tongue* in Persian?
It is *tong* / *tonge* / tongs in Afrikaans—
lick knife of meaning with flaming imprecision.
The impression this poem harbours
is the tip of its protracted U reaching out
into the expanse of lingual lengthening, lingering
and then eliminating dissection in lieu
of a decorative ribbon sailing endlessly into in.

---

za-bunn زبان *(Persian) tongue*
tong (Afrikaans) tongue
tonge (Afrikaans) tongues

prosTHETIC

When we part what do I take away from you?
When we part what is shared between us?
What has been severed from one to be left with the other?
I once told an elder that his language had roots in mine
not as historical one-upmanship, but as a connection
culturally severed and assimilated
into a language he refused to share with mine
like I refuse to reconcile my tongue with the Ancient
                    Greeks.
A prosthetic for?   Or prosthetic to?
To annex a bodiless organ into a system
perhaps the mind wants to jump
from prosthesis to artifice
to organ, callous
a teethening of thesis

my mother tongue aching in yours:

                             phantom pain

when words are shared
and your roots become my creole.
Pain is felt not in bodily apparatus
but in the echoplex of history—
my history becomes "borrowed"
from *aari* to *aarie*
a *saaz* now *saagté*

     sagte.

We begin with feet planted in soil unclear on distance.
We use ancestry as a ruler to measure how deep feet can sink.

----

aari عاری *(Persian) exempt*
aarie عاریه *(Persian) borrowed*
saaz ساز *(Persian) instrument, and vocative for the verb construct*
saagté ساخته *(Persian) construct*
sagte (Afrikaans) soft
sagte (German) said

PROSthetic

Cursive *I*,   water
                  cascading
cursivus as in smokestacks and antennae
bent at the kissing point of mother tongue
and the vernacular,   the speech-bubble burst
freudian
slippery recess of the libido
surfacing
////////
there is /
the /
I /
of /
the language-cyclone /
           violently swirling
                  / into meaning
                        / where one situates
                              / the self is arbitrary
           \ direction is arbitrary \   / one is always defined
        \ position is prosthetic / an I \   / by the distance
\ the event horizon   / inside \   / the *I* of the storm
        \ words into   / an eye \   / to swirling arms: *pros*thetic
           \ pushing   ◎ / the vacuous centre
                  \ violently swallowing.

Vestigium

Anxiety leaves a trace in my throat that wakes me up
     folding onto language is a painful process
pain's a little neuron ladder of words
but anxiety's a late stage simulacrum
of all the nothingness to come
so I ink the *être* in my poetrey
and live in the vestigium
of all that speech denies me.
I wake up to a new utterance of myself
     somewhere I've read that teleportation
     annihilates the traveller / reconstructs
and I'm wondering if these letters keep their meaning
in tomorrow's utterance of self?
Utter like to utt past participle utté
tossing word salad on the tongue
(the psyche has its own immune system)
the key is repeating words into primal abstraction
don't take yourself too seriously
let words stare.

Who was it who said language
was a virus? ...
                    Oh yes fear
      that proxy warmonger
      arming words
      so death can sleep
      blossoming
      blooming
      blighted
      rapid chlorosis
   an imago of the eternal
   nestled in thoughts
  themselves nestled
in words.

être (French) be

G

The [χ] trapped in my throat
like *geld*, phlegm rattling
  variegated leaves
stuck
my larynx
my coniferous *g*

[χ] (phonetic alphabet) shared non-sibilant fricative sound in
    Afrikaans and Persian
geld خلط *(Persian) phlegm*
geld (Afrikaans) money; apply; be valid

Gelding is a violent art.
Roots of the tongue lie,
two round nouns in a bowl.

Geld, geldig, geldigheid.
Soft cough.

The throat, a line like a strophe
applying its orientation
to the vertical verb of the torso.

---

geld (Afrikaans) money; apply; be valid
geldig (Afrikaans) valid
geldigheid (Afrikaans) validity

g [χ] غ
g [χ] غ
g [χ] غ
g [χ] غ
g [χ] غ
g [χ] غ
g [χ] غ
g [χ] غ
g [χ] غ
g [χ] غ
g [χ] غ
g [χ] غ
g [χ] غ
g [χ] غ

[χ] *(phonetic alphabet) shared non-sibilant fricative sound in Afrikaans and Persian*

غ *(Persian) fricative corresponding to g in Afrikaans and* [χ] *in phonetic alphabet*

An *Oχ* and
a herd of oxen
pass by,
syncopate
their hooves
in the mooing.
The upholstered air
squeezes hot
microscopic drops
from the sky while
*Oχ*en lug legs
through the *lug,*
air cattle
tended by an inner
longing to talk,
therapeutic horde.

---

oχ خٰ¹ (Persian) ouch
lug (Afrikaans) air; sky

Oχ
Ox
Oksel
Oxygen

---

oχ خٰ (Persian) ouch
oksel (Afrikaans) armpit

Two sentry I
        and I echo
the pressure of f I nger upon fist
        the bod I ly vibrations of language
                m I ddle toes
        as certa I n sounds leave the larynx
                Oχ! l I ke Ouch! as in
                        I ache
        on either s I de of the
                        I
                a thou I n the
                        m I rror
                        χ*ash*
                        χ*eesh* / *god*
the first syllable
a   stylus
scratching
a   *gash*
    or *god*
\\\\\ progenitor
   \\\ of the thought-ladder
     \ exploding
            into
binary
                    fractals

---

*o*χ آخ *(Persian) ouch*
χ*ash*/*gash* خش *(Persian) scratch*
χ*eesh*/*geesh* خویش *(Persian) self*
χ*od*/*god* خود *(Persian) self*
god (Afrikaans) god

26

The binary is a tactile shade
in which the body is cast
sometimes unwillingly,
sometimes caught
up in itself.

This us,
this me-and-you
poem resides in the we
ons / maw / of our mouths
languaging the ego into abstraction.

---

ons (Afrikaans) we
maw مه (Persian) us
maw (Afrikaans) abbreviation for "met ander woorde" in other words

maw	we	
maw	mouth	
maw	*met ander woorde*	in other words

---

maw مَا *(Persian) us*
maw (Afrikaans) abbreviation for "met ander woorde" in other words

The mouth is a land-locked organ   *mond*
opening into air,
in other words,
the mouth is a coastal organ   *monding*
expressing itself into water known as air,
in other words,
sky inlets enter the body
that is land, that is being,   *mond ding*
in other words,
words and air trade
is
for
is
in the soft airstrip of in-between   *mondig*

---

mond (Afrikaans) mouth
monding (Afrikaans) estuary
mond ding (Afrikaans) mouth thing
mondig (Afrikaans) of age
is (Afrikaans) is

Lang-locked   far from the tongue-tip
you are now where language no longer serves you
  have passed the threshold of self-serving continuity
when you sleep on your χ   you wake
χ*ar dar galoo.*   Your own body   in pursuit
of inhalation   the body can only express   by expanding
  we are past signifier and signified now   downing
    the pursuit of gender   before finding an answer
      to words themselves.   The desire to know
              what is a (wo)man / before knowing
                      what is a what
                          what
                            is
                            an
                              is

χ*ar dar galoo* خار در گلو *(Persian) idiomatic, tongue-tied; literally,*
  thorn in the throat

Ast as the difference between is and *is*.

Ast	Asterisk
Aste	Astern
Aster	Aster
Astrant	*Ast*

Is　　*ast*　*is*

---

ast است *(Persian) is*
is (Afrikaans) is
aste (Afrikaans) used as in "so nooit aste nimmer"; never
aster (Afrikaans) chrysanthemum
astrant (Afrikaans) cheeky; impudent

e(*Ast*) to w'*Est*
dis'*Ast*-er   *mal-Aχtar*
northernstarletmold
cometscreenwipe the sky

---

ast است *(Persian) is*
est (French) is; east
mal (French) bad
aχtar اختر *(Persian) star*

Is   *hast*
be-*hast*   be-hest
be-hes(h)t   best
he *hast*   *behesht*
hy haat   heaven
s/he *hast* the *ha(s)te(h)*
of being.

---

hast هست (Persian) *is*
hast (German) *has; hates*
behesht بهشت (Persian) *heaven; va-heesh-taw (Avestan roots) best,*
    kinship with English best
he hast behesht (German-Persian pun) he is heaven; he hates heaven
hy haat (Afrikaans) he hates
hy haat هیهات *(Persian) how far it is*
hasteh هسته *(Persian) core; centre*

For Joseph Ianni

Existence
ex-*hast*-ence
exhausted
n'est-ed within
      ast
hasty   *est*-itude
c'est/uaries
po-*est*:po-is
po-ette:po-*ek*
po-*être* cum po-*écriture*
po-*etriture*
        is
peut-etriture.

---

hast (German) has
hast هست *(Persian) is*
n'est (French) is not
est (French) is; east
ast است *(Persian) is*
hasty هستى *(Persian) existence*
c'est (French) it is
ek (Afrikaans) I
être (French) be
écriture (French) writing
peut-être (French) maybe

34

Nestle in words like an animal
mythologizing and severing
nature into morality. The antler
that gores, accidentally healing
a nail, a tooth, a horn.
The callous tip that roots into viscera
or the hoof, thickened into prosthesis.
Animal-mythos clashing
with the next door neighbour's
worship. Language as natural mythos
agglutinated, the *gorg o meesh* of speech.

---

gorg o meesh گرگ و میش *(Persian) twilight; literally, wolf and sheep; the time of daylight during which a wolf is indistinguishable from a sheep*

The sun-matched sea
water-coloured by sky
gold sunbeams
augmenting vision
surface compounded
with marble-glare.

Tongue-tipped words
filtered through waterfalls.
Building block of two tongues
agglutinated until illegible.
Speech is surface-tense.
It lies on the superfice.

Under the viscous surface
of all that is written
lies the puritanical tongue
of the non-referential.
The mouth as bulwark
guarding the sleep-tongue
from spilling into waking life.

Language names itself
discusses itself
moves in registers in relation to itself
but doesn't recognize itself
by name
so never calls itself
language. It isn't good with names
it subsumes and begets itself anew
healing a death-consonant
between vowels
con-sonare   con-sonant with
(nasal)   (lateral)
never to speak again.

Words as trace
objects made
from oeuvrelessness—
the footprint
of imagery
made distinct
by memory.

Towards
To words

Dwelling
        in *haw-shieh*
a widening margin means
I can breathe in language again
but   not all fricatives scratch
some foam at the diastema
distant travellers
from heat
to callous chill
of cliffs.
Each sh is a wave that breaks
pebbles underneath the incisor
                  dandoon neesh
                  shab-poosh
and the page is swept under the poem
hush hush full-moonlit poem hush hush.

---

haw-shieh حاشیه *(Persian) margin*
dandoon neesh دندون نیش *(Persian) incisor; literally, stinger tooth*
shab-poosh شب پوش *(Persian) nightclad*

My poem has been distanced from the tortoise-shell lyre
it doesn't educate / it doesn't rhyme / it's not mnemonic
my language is not accessible through the ear /   my
language is not even my language /   it has absorbed
too much to be on its own /   how can my words be
any less just by expanding /   why am I excommunicated
for pronouncing diphthongs here /   excommunicated
for trilling my r there /   silly how we
soften the consonants for some /   harden them
for others /   a game of nationalities   we
sand the edges to appeal /   play with our tongue
a language does not harshen with a χ /   its kinesis
instead folds back into the throat as warmth / we soften
words into English /   unwilling /   names
disappear   cultures   fade
into   geo   -graphy

borders sharpied onto our tongues till unhinged / till unfit for the frame.

My poem is a shard.
This poem is a sharing. Against all odds
share is poem in Persian.

So I *share*
and you *share*
and we *share*
in this sheer fantasy of names,
overlaid and veiled.
Word mask that peers
through the heart of language, across layers
scars / *skaars* / *skare* cheering us on.
We cherrypick lustre,
but the endlessly long fingertips of language
undulate and snap.

I shear the poem in two and then mend it.

---

share شعر *(Persian) poem*
skaars (Afrikaans) scarce; barely
skare (Afrikaans) crowd; mob

ge-dig
ge-dic(h)t
ge-nicht
ge-nist

---

ge- (Afrikaans) prefix for past tense formation
dig (Afrikaans) write poetry
gedig (Afrikaans) poem
Gedicht (German) poem
nicht (German) not
Ge-nicht (German) Paul Celan's play on "Gedicht," often translated
 as "no-em"
nist نیست *(Persian) non-existent*

[*Slap* is flaccid
like a body
ragdolling   in *slaap*
reason
ge-(dig) de-duct
Paleo-*dig*-o-graph
        de-scribed
        and
        sorg-ening

Flaxen slap
like a boy
lolling on his back in sleep.
He's deduced a digging
graphically descried
in
the field of sorghum.]

---

slap (Afrikaans) flaccid; loose
slaap (Afrikaans) sleep
ge- (Afrikaans) prefix for past tense formation
dig (Afrikaans) write poetry
gedig (Afrikaans) poem
sorg (Afrikaans) care; worry
sorg سرخ (Persian) red

Ur-text
of this composition
lithography orthography / prehistoric
stone words

oer outeur intones long voices
bone groove vowel / *vokaal* / vocal

actually *klinkers* (clink click)
cinch the text along its torso, A-line
at the widest substrate of the upper body.

The adult body is an outmoded script
shuddering in assonance
rolled up like a rug
with runs tearing down its limbs
and urns to support its indignation.

---

oer (Afrikaans) prehistoric; archetypal
outeur (Afrikaans) author
vokaal (Afrikaans) vowel; vocal
klinkers (Afrikaans) vowels

ggggggggggggggggggggggggggg
ggggggggggggggggggggggggggg
ggggggggggggggggggggggggggg
ggggggggggggggggggggggggggg
ggggggggggggggggggggggggggg
ggggggggggggggggggggggggggg
ggggggggggggggggggggggggggg
ggggggggggggggggggggggggggg
ggggggggggggggggggggggggggg
ggggggggggggggggggggggggggg
ggggggggggggggggggggggggggg
ggggggggggggggggggggggggggg
ggggggggggggggggggggggggggg
ggggggggggggggggggggggggggg

The past tense *ge-* is its own friction / fricative.

---

ge- (Afrikaans) prefix for past tense formation

Past tense *ge-*
Present tense *gedig*

Present tense dig
Past tense dug

*Ge-*dig
Dig the poem / *gedug*

Dug the poem
Gedugte digter

Daunting poet
Poets 'n gedig

Present tense *dig*
To compose a poem

Past tense *gedig*
To have composed

Present tense *gedig*
Past tense *ge-*

---

ge- (Afrikaans) prefix for past tense formation
gedig (Afrikaans) poem
gedug, gedugte (Afrikaans) daunting; formidable
digter (Afrikaans) poet
poets 'n gedig (Afrikaans) polish a poem
dig (Afrikaans) write poetry

Breath becomes breathe
and spit becomes spirit.
Just like giving up the ghost   *gee die gees*
lets geese take wing
as if wings were for the taking

One wing is
-ing and and the other *ge-*
verb becoming noun and   *gees gegee*
noun becoming past
continuity, an asymmetry

of wings and lungs
lunging along the migratory
patterns of the chest.   *heilige gees*
Wings grafted to the back,
breathing the outer air.

---

gee die gees (Afrikaans) give up the ghost / spirit; die
ge- (Afrikaans) prefix for past tense formation
gees gegee (Afrikaans) gave up the ghost / spirit; energize
heilige gees (Afrikaans) holy ghost / spirit

god is self
and
man is me

how Persian
transforms
my sense   of being.

---

god (Afrikaans) god
god خود (Persian) self
man (Afrikaans) man
man من: (Persian) me

Man am

---

man am منم *(Persian) it is I*

                    Teeth
shatter
          covered with sawdust
                    a
gnaw can deny
that being can become
non-being
from *bood* to *gnaw-bood*
                    a
nihilo can become
annihilated
from *heech*
          to *fa(gnaw)*
there is no limit
to how far
the nothingness can stretch
the entirety of language
spherical stacking   / much
space left between building blocks
                    eyes
don't sway into dreams easily
when there's a ceiling
visibly towering above
sightlines escape
unyielding to sleep:
                    the only
                              respite
                              from
                              language.

---

gnaw نا (Persian) *prefix for non-*
bood بود (Persian) *existent*
gnaw-bood نابود (Persian) *non-existent; annihilated*
heech هیچ (Persian) *nothing; nothingness*
fa-gnaw فنا (Persian) *Sufi term for annihilation*

Fricatives recline in their resonance
across languages and landscapes /
landskappe en tongskappe /
vibrating at the frequency of speech.

The thing about expansiveness
is that it never comes to an end / *einder*
being a placeholder for the line of sight
circling around continents / consonants
Thrill-seeking and trilling.

Each word sinks beneath the horizon
of its throat. Oral moon leaves one last ovum
glimmering in the nighttime stratum
of the sentence. Straddling grammar,
the egg / *eier / eie / ei /* staggers inside its own
weight, the shell needling its decline
with the technology of a crack.

Sin / sinful / *sonde / sondage*
see, a survey of sounds
shows a sensational reliance on similarity,
on familiarity, intimacy, coitus interruptus,
on a firm verbal handshake shivering
across the surface of poems, loanwords,
and dictionaries in all languages.

Dipping in and out of relevance /
reverb fricative / returns with daybreak /
line break / crisps diction with gruff
crackling of spikes, spittle, and frills.

To separate a sound into functionality,
then to reunite it with gentle endlessness /
langskap einders / of lungscapes.

———————————————

landskappe (Afrikaans) landscapes
en (Afrikaans) and
tongskappe (Afrikaans) neologism, tonguescapes
einder (Afrikaans) horizon
eier (Afrikaans) egg
eie (Afrikaans) own
ei (Afrikaans) used as in "'n appel en 'n ei"; for a mere song
sin (Afrikaans) sentence; sense
sonde (Afrikaans) sin
sondage (French) survey
langskap (Afrikaans) neologism, longscape
einders (Afrikaans) horizons

Vawhed now *vawheh*
from *toheed* to *tohee*
the tongue is prosthetic unity
pros- : *in addition to*
+τίθημι : to put (literal act of laying down)
like τίθημῐ πόδα : I plant the foot
τίθημῐ τὰ ὅπλα:

>> I rest arms
>> I bear arms
>> I lay down arms and surrender

language is pros-θέσις
an addition seeking to fulfil
an absent limb   itching
a primal map   ejaculate from
a time-bruise on the throat.
The last song beyond mankind
words as habitat for a thought system
systemic erasure of sounds
the k now silent in knife
the performative exploitation
of sounds lost to history
q(u')es(t-ce) q(u)e c'e(st)
(g)nostic tho(ugh)t apropo(s) bigbang ex nihilo
phlegm's elusive g
the χ of Afrikaans
geld in throat
lifted off to spell
the letter that sands
my tongue-root

there are too many moving parts to the self
the only continuity is through language .
there is an entropy to friction
feel its lucidity
say χ and listen
to its pulse
climb out.

---

vawhed واحد *(Arabic) unit*
vawheh واحه *(Persian) oasis*
toheed توحید *(Arabic) unity*
tah ته *(Persian) end*
tohee تهی *(Persian) empty; literally, that without an end; endless*
tithenai τίθημι *(Greek) put; literally, the act of lying down*
tithnyi poda τίθημῐ πόδα *(Greek) plant the foot*
tithnyi ta opda τίθημῐ τὰ ὅπλα *(Greek) I bear arms*
thesis θέσις *(Greek) thesis*
q'est-ce que c'est (French) what is it
geld خلط *(Persian) phlegm*
geld (Afrikaans) money; to apply; to be valid

"The last song beyond mankind" is a reference to Paul Celan's
Threadsuns (Fadensonnen).

Speech

Speech:

aaaaa$_a$^{a}aa$_a$aaa^{a}a^{aa}aaaaaaa^{aaa}
my serrated throat:

                        modular
khk$_{hkh}$^{i}u^{khk}hakhio^{k}h$_{kh}$ukhio
needing a bass drum
ploded behind the mic
P.

        /   P.

thoroughly percussed
in the images it takes
to arrive at the word.
I was quoted and I quoted.
When I got to fingers that smell
there was an aversion
see there's a corner of language | where
I've ordered us to stay in speech.
I've ordered us two glasses of wine.
Quarter plosives on the quarter beat
P.

        /   P.

| o | o | o | o |
            fricatives in the quarter tone
amassed scales beyond the anglo
and all the otherwise perceived ones.
Ok... look: I've said this before:
when I speak as I'm spoken to
a new effort emerges
from
khk$_{hkh}$^{i}u^{k}h$_{kh}$akhio^{k}h$_k$^{hu}khio

My silence finds that quarter attractive.
My silence smells of fingers
no matter how far.
                    Listen:
when first put into the frame
the letter shakes
a *harf*
is the letter written, a unit or a stage
is the sentence uttered, a hammer or the mouth
is speech
is listen: is key.
Listen! Speech must have
at least a rasp
of what we write.
The affricate fits nice in the fist.
The fricative dislocates the jaw.
The affricate fits in teeth.
Only fricatives can
        (through practice)
        clarify.

---

harf حرف *(Persian) letter; speech*

Poems in the *Speech* section were composed out loud and tran-
scribed, rather than written down. The opening lines break out
into sound as an informal gesture away from the printed word.

Speech:

For Xin Wang

Face-to-face, the soprano
tells me my voice is harmonic
tells me my voice is consistently two:
deeper base   airy and dependent
  base strand   higher
      hammer   I am
between neck and throat
the slit of musical ventilation
voicing a constant split. She says,
I have never heard this so consistently
in a voice, but, she says, listening
before the sound is the best listening.
I contract my own soprano
stinging flute voice
high heightened register
agency of singing in such I, I
I am my own throat
its walls
the lynx of larynx slinking
along the hollow organ. But if I
have learned anything
it's that emptiness is always presence
that the hollow is its own muscle.
When my gruff voice grovels | gravels | gavels
I crack open the fricative
of my citational Africa
road tongues constantly
expulsing earth breath
into the language of my body
of my story

of my stones, bones, gasping tone.
I who am also l who is also 1 who is also |
I line my litany
a line
align
a lie
recline in the shadow of this speech
in the gasp of this poem
shuddering forth from affricate togetherness.

Lecture addressed
to all vocalists
all soloists
in rogue monologue
in soaring fury
that this rhyme
this relentless, beckoning roar
is stranded in the open poem
agoraphobic
erotic glottis
of neckline.

Speech:

Flute voices
Stone base
Teeth in mortar
So… carried away
To dream-charred speech
      Gone
      Speaking louder than
      The soprano
      And spoken louder to
(it's a term in the sublingual dissolve!)
Your recline and my linguistic incline
Only dissected in the dreamtongue
Y'know…
When you
Speak too
Much you
Repeat…
And when you repeat yourself you're
        Insisting
      There's a tremor
      Like a library chair shifting
      A single floor above
      Squeaking under my tongue
    Squeegee the shelf at either end
Of my speech and a shell: a shelf: alive
The singularity of laughter inside
The laugh-out-loud archive
Little talons of speech little
Electric nights of spooning
The tongue and waking up
      Skinned

I always begin
With so much damn ambition
I'm talking to you but believe me on the page
I'm SPEAKING not writing and waking up.
Believe me I can't sleep on the other side of the tongue!
Believe me next time we collide.
I can. Talk without moving. But can't move.
I can. Laugh without moving. But can't move.
A third of life in my hands when I am beyond the divide
Wait a minute! Did I ever tell you we were roommates with a curtain as a divide?
Did I ever tell you you can peek through no matter what I'm doing on the other side
Ok. They all begin weird like this.
What can I do about speech but gear up
With breath and subdued self
Breath and breath-crumbs
In- and sub- dividual.
Lemme see! I wanna see!
I keep telling you I don't know the depth
Of what's lost in writing.
The micro dissolved
Kham like the *khatkesh*
Khurush az khame charkha chachi bekhaast
                    A litter of alliteration
Investing in rasping of bows and roaring of arrows

I lick with my serrated tongue this envelope that holds
Every letter and a letter to you
> *Sholoogh*
> Like the streets with
> policy
> Like the store with
> customers
> How many wars ago was this before the
> divide?
> *Enghelaab*: from Usurp to Revolution
> Remember the dead? We'll say one day
> Remembering numbers
> But not names
> Not the line

---

kham خم: *(Persian) bend*
khatkesh خط‌کش *(Persian) ruler*
khurush az khame charkha chachi bekhaast خروش از خم چرخ چاچی بخاست
(Persian) a line of alliteration in Ferdowsi's Shahnameh, *using the tremor*
  of kh and sh to invoke the strength of a bow being drawn to its very limits
sholoogh شلوغ *(Persian) busy; crowded*
enghelaab انقلاب *(Persian) revolution*

Speech:

What is this speech anyway?
The abstraction of language
or the words
        in | out
             of my mouth
        in | out
             of my mind
question mark
        in | in
question mark
        out | out
speech reversing to suck monologue
deep into the gag reflex of transcription.
        mouth
        moth
        mother
Did I ever tell you that I am the curtain?
fluttering and fluctuating with my one single wing

Speech:

On meeting one of my favourite artists
I say, no, no, I cannot shake
you by the hand. I cannot partake
in this wringing connection,
this sociability of anxiety.
Suturing fingers.
This is not beyond the social.
This is not anti-gestural.
Wet language of the mouth
hand-hand coordination
letting go of the clasp, gasping
through orifice of face-off.
Excuse me, I don't like meeting with hands.
I commune with mouth,
speech leaking from lip squeeze.
Why am I so cold?
Why am I so sultry?
Instinctively my hands eliminate themselves
into lyrics,
lyrical speakers.
They are themselves in the distance between symmetry.
The definitions of poetry become the author
I can never be
not for silence
but for the manual labour of language.

To be pinned down in the catastrophic garment of being.
Burdened and bedded with voice.
I hand my hands to the artist.
Within the exoskeleton of speech,
of giftgiving, of yes, here, please,
I regress into a redness so potent
that the tips of my life are reborn.

Speech:

The conversation shifts colours
shifts down
to a single unit of speech.

Ok.
See...
The length of emphasis
and a question of
repetition
            a question
            framing
Harf
        or *Kalaam*

Ok.
You.
Didn't.
Like it.

I farm Persian rugs
for their rose blossoms
to hack at my subconscious
like a scribe.

Ok.
See...
My greatest obstacle to speaking
is wave after wave of spit
breaking on the tongue

harf حرف *(Persian) letter; speech*
kalaam كلام *(Persian) speech; language*

Speech:

I implore you to read the instructions out loud.
I ask of speech to bubble outside the head
and never inside.

Aw! So cute!
Is it an indoor
or an outdoor phrase?

Of course we repeat ourselves
because language repeats itself.
Of course I keep rethinking apparatus
because Klara
because only Klara
and if Klara
and "if" or "and"
is a thoughtseam
that speech will defy
in its generous blades
scalpels for the idiolexicon.

Listen!
If you're tired of all the iterations
                of "listen"
you need to remember
I'm spoken in delight.

K Klara K Khashayar
we crash
into the poem
razed ledges and raised tongues
retroflex but still rasping
in this pulmonic little sound.

Listen to the
Speech:
and remember
it'll be followed
by more **Speech:**

Speech:
punctuation puncture
bring percussion
blue the lip wide
blue the ear to the side
Speech:
down the puncture
up and through the eye
sub-lingus sub-contracted
sub-liminal .
with floating ⁱ heads and
floating   i
pulled tongue, braised tongue
do it for the space of the divide
do it for the separations
and the immovable
and the conscience
and the heartstring
and the cold tongue on
                    dinner night
do it for the speaker
speaking that:

Speech:

Is it
ok
OK
okay?

Or just K?
~~Khashayar~~ | ~~Klara~~

If this speech were address,
my head would angle
towards you
and say

If this poem were apostrophe
I'd angel up
on the apparatus of my speech
and turn

to shout
okay
OK
ok
exclamations clamouring
at porticoes
of poem noise.
Swap any word for poem
I | poem
am | poem
I am | poem poem
what is this | poem poem poem
the whole huge poem
engulfs an epic wave of language, ok,

but more than that,
poemness infiltrating, filtering, flitting through filigree.
Unpunctuated aaaahhhh!!!! of poetry
the loosening
the letting go
the letting through
exactly in the instant when I | poem |
I hope that when the poem poems the poem out loud
I will physically shriek at the only instance of
punctuation
I have ever allowed myself,
separating,
clarifying,
silken, baby, fetus of being,
threading in the shivering thriving of ok.

If I were speech
less clench
more outing.
The way my mouth elongates as lateral signing
when I say
ok
OK
okay
this poem was supposed to invoke
to splay
to say
collateral collaboration
guttural
gut
urethra of linguistic longing pulsing
up the vibrating slit
between vocal cords and vocal folds
voluptuous luxury

draping
am-ing about.
I am the poem | I hate | I love poem poem poem
equally sarcophagus as esophagus,
citational shout of inscription,
muscular tube of saying out, saying out loud, aloud, allowed
trinity of sphincters
ascending the throat
to | towards | to words

o
O
Oh POEM

Note on Transliteration

Functioning through the connective tissue of English, *G*'s translingualism runs on a dual axis of Persian and Afrikaans. For Persian, a practice of transliteration was applied, one relying on non-standard, sonic approximations. The goal was both to amplify and destabilize semantic connections through homonymic intersections between languages, even when this implied gently stretching words to bring them into closer relation to one another. With a few exceptions, Arabic script resides in the translation sections. In contrast, Afrikaans shares the Roman alphabet with English and so retains its standardized spelling. While this slight variation in translingual approach is suggestive of a different dynamic between the languages collectively, the progression of linguistic sonic playfulness remains consistent throughout this collaborative collection.

Note on Collaboration

The substantial section, "G," was written over the course of a few months in a burst of interwoven, collaborative composition. The process was so reciprocal and co-dependent that the poets can't always remember who wrote what. In contrast, "زبان" and "Speech" were produced in a different mode: although the poets sent poems back and forth and developed writing from the energy of preceding works, they experience the resulting poems as more discernibly authored. Khashayar "Kess" Mohammadi wrote the poems "prosTHETIC," "PROSthetic," and "Vestigium," as well as those starting "aaaaaaaaaaaaa," "Flute voices," "The conversation shifts colours," and "I implore you." Klara du Plessis composed "پروتز," "Prostese," "Kuns-," and "Tongs," and those with first lines "Face-to-face," "What is this speech anyway?," "On meeting one of my favourite artists," and "Is it / ok."

Acknowledgements

Poems from "G" were published as "Four Poems" in *The Capilano Review,* Translingual / Fall Issue 2020.

A sound work based on extracts and versions from "G" was published as a digital feature called "Fricatives" in *Collusion Books' 2×4^2* series, 2021.
longconmag.com/collusionbooks/digital/2x4two/fricatives

A version of a poem from "G" was published as "Fricative 20" in *Shrapnel Magazine,* 2 May 2021. https://www.shrapnelmagazine.com/poetry/fricative-20?rq=mohammadi

A sound work based on extracts and versions from "G" was published as a digital performance through the TAP Centre for Creativity's 42 x 81 series, January 2022.
tapcreativity.org/42x81/khashayar-mohammadi-and-klara-du-plessis

"پروتز," "Kuns-," and "PROSthetic" were published in *Grain Magazine,* 50th Anniversary Issue, 2023.

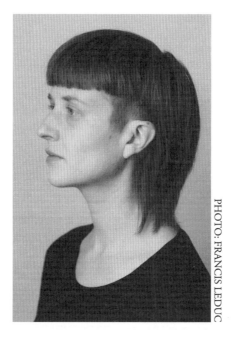

Klara du Plessis is a poet, scholar, and literary curator. Her debut poetry collection, *Ekke,* won the 2019 Pat Lowther Memorial Award and her critical writing received *Arc Poetry Magazine*'s 2022 Critic's Desk Award. Welcoming collaborative formations, her book-length narrative poem, *Hell Light Flesh*, was adapted and produced as a mono-opera film with composer Jimmie LeBlanc, premiered at the International Festival of Films on Art (FIFA) in 2023. Klara develops an ongoing series of experimental and dialogic literary events called Deep Curation, an approach which posits the poetry reading as artform. She holds a PhD in English Literature, and lives in Montreal.

PHOTO: TRAM NGHIEM

Khashayar "Kess" Mohammadi is a nonbinary, Iranian-born, Toronto-based poet, writer, and translator. They were short-listed for the 2021 Austin Clarke Prize in Literary Excellence, the 2022 *Arc Poetry Magazine* Poem of the Year Award, the 2023 *PRISM* Open Season Awards, and they are the winner of the 2021 *Vallum* Poetry Award. They are the author of four poetry chapbooks and three translated poetry chapbooks. They have released two full-length collections of poetry with Gordon Hill Press. Their collection of experimental dream-poems, *Daffod*ls*, is forthcoming from Pamenar Press, Fall 2023.